Kitchen, 12.07 a.m.

Julian Flanagan

KITCHEN, 12.07 a.m.

Kitchen, 12.07 a.m.
Published in the United Kingdom in 2018
by Mica Press

c/o Leslie Bell, 47 Belle Vue Road, Wivenhoe,
Colchester, Essex, CO7 9LD, U.K.
www.micapress.co.uk | books@micapress.co.uk

ISBN 978-1-869848-22-4

Copyright © Julian Flanagan 2018

The right of Julian Flanagan to be identified as the author of this work has been asserted by him in accordance with the Copyright, Designs and Patents Act of 1988.

All rights reserved.

Acknowledgements

The following poems first appeared in the following publications:

'Call it a Night', *Envoi* 118; 'Moving Away', *The Interpreter's House*, Issue 49; 'Dirty Washing', *The Spectator*, 14 November 1992; 'Still Up', *Obsessed with Pipework*, Issue 17, Winter 2001-2; 'Insect Noise, Jamaica' and 'Susan on the Wharf', *Ambit* 169; 'The Toy Man', *Envoi* 118; 'End and Beginning', *The Penniless Press,* Issue 15; 'Side Order', *Envoi* 118; 'For Madeleine Mulcahey, 16 July 1998 - 17 December 2000', *Seam*, Issue 17; 'The Drunk's Stigmata', *Envoi* 118; 'Small Autumn', *Smoke*, Issue 43; 'By the Kitchen Door', *The Reader*, Issue 67; 'Evening Flight, Kingston-London', *The Reader*, Issue 58; 'For Miss Esther Small', *Obsessed with Pipework*, Issue 16, Autumn 2001; 'News From Afghanistan', *Envoi* 118; 'Key to a Map', 'The Domesday Book Entry for High Legh Village', and 'Sanctuary Wood', *The Manchester Review*, Issue 13; 'Retiring', *Skylight 47*, Issue 10; 'Keltneyburn Again', *Tandem*, Issue 4/5.

The author photograph on the back cover is by Eleanor Flanagan and the front cover photograph is by Delia Ridley-Thomas.

To Caroline,
at the circus, and everywhere else.

Kitchen, 12.07 a.m.

Call it a Night	1
Moving Away	2
New Born Winter	3
Dirty Washing	4
Hello Love	5
Still Up	6
Insect Noise, Jamaica	7
The Toy Man	8
End and Beginning	9
Side Order	10
Kitab suwar al-kawakib (Book of the Constellations of the Fixed Stars)	11
For Madeleine Mulcahey, 16 July 1998 – 17 December 2000	12
The Drunk's Stigmata	13
Kitchen, 12.07 a.m.	14
Somewhere There	15
Small Autumn	16
Smoke Signals	17
By the Kitchen Door	18
Evening Flight, Kingston–London	19
For Miss Esther Small	20
News From Afghanistan	21
A Long Line	22
Key to a Map	23
Surprise Incarnation	24
Two Dreaming Queens	25
Edward Hopper in Harrogate	26

High Definition	27
Retiring	28
Tough	29
Cathedral City	30
To My Wife, at the Circus	31
The Domesday Book Entry for High Legh Village	32
Keltneyburn Again	33
Elusive Spin	34
Relic	35
From the Tribal Homelands	36
Christmas in Isolation	37
Out of Touch	38
Unfinished Business	39
A Taxi Driver Named Ahmed	40
Sanctuary Wood	41
Susan on the Wharf	42
Is That the Time Already?	43
Apart	44
Travelling Companions	45
Restoring Balance	47
San Trovarso, Venice, in the District of Dorsoduro	48

Call it a Night

It must be five now,
so this lightening can't only be
the street lamps' yellow bruise.

Even the silence is exhausted
as birds tune in
for the morning show.

Inside, Ben, Ejiro and Paul
have already laid themselves down,
like a modest cellar, under the dining room table.

I'll leave them
to the cold becoming fresher
and prepare to regret the Drambuie and mead.

Moving Away

Our first roll of honeymoon snaps
is haunted by double exposures
and the wedding guests gatecrash Venice:
friends stand knee-deep in a piazza,
cousins party in relic-heavy churches,
a flotilla of aunts hang in mid-canal.

Then Verona, Florence, a new roll
and Caroline sits at an open book,
bella figura in black polo neck,
the old convent balcony behind her
empty of new ghosts.

New Born Winter

Four days out of the water,
Alice leads us into the submariner's life.
Behind the front door's Banham hatch,
radiators click on 24-hour duty,
the pressed stack of nappies on standby.
At night, parched soundings alert Caroline.
She sits up to feed,
back against five torpedo pillows,
the nightlight and mumbling World Service attendant.

By day we walk the wooden-decked dining room,
Alice cuttle-fished in a white blanket.
Outside, currents shift
the trees' alarmed branches
and shoals of late leaves.
Alice opens her eyes,
sly as periscopes,
and, sighting so much land, shuts them.
Her empty lips twitch for the soft scuba of a breast.

Dirty Washing

You squat for this,
squat and squeeze the obedient stud,
bursting the porthole like a mantrap,
the soft rubber lips
O so astonished at their work
and now blowing cold.

Then you pull the damp massacre
from the chamber
(the arms around each other,
the twisted legs bent under,
the socks lolling like tongues)
and sort them,
back against the oven door.

Hello Love

A ninety something silence in the front room at
                                    Kimberley Street,
Aunt Kate defined great age.
The room opened off the tarred street,
one square of the Battenberg-neat two up two down.
From a shrinkage of zippered slippers and a flock of wool,
she'd be watching the telly from the side
which she thought better:
you could see the off-screen action too.
I'd kiss her cheek, unsure if she knew who I was;
but she'd smile, kiss, nod.

In the next room would come
Aunty Lily's spread-arms "He-llo love!"
Uncle George's unshaven hug,
Our Lady of Lourdes keeping order
from her china grotto above the fire,
the hope of a sugar sandwich.

But here, Aunt Kate,
a steel wool will
disguised as crocheted fuzz,
moon shots, homburged Chancellors,
tidal hemlines on
from turning down the farmer's proposal,
rationing life to raising her dead brother's
Lily, Polly, Tom and Martin,
keeping them where she could see them,
safe from any off-screen action.

Still Up

The night crop of silence
is stacked over High Legh,
the lanes and side woods,
fields and sunken meres.
Our house creaks under it:
beams shrink just slightly,
heavy-footed wardrobes tick politely,
Alice's busy sleep shuffles through the baby alarm.

The plot is bound in hawthorn
and, so, witch-proof,
and the monochrome garden
can go about its noiseless business undisturbed.
Low apple trees scrum down.
Old pigsties lurk,
beady as pillboxes in the rhododendrons.
The willow gleans the rough grass.

Damson trees border the lawn,
their oval leaves hanging down,
pleading innocence – we have nothing.
But look inside, up at the brittle web
and find their fruit of small nights,
clouding over now
with a cirrus of sugar under the skin,
ready for the step ladder and tomorrow's picking pot.

Insect Noise, Jamaica

A lawnmower is cutting lanes
through the stairwell's plot of air.
Outside, B-Feature UFOs
whirr invisibly all the fat afternoon.
They rise slowly in saucer-spread branches
to hover at full throttle.

And at supper,
past the rim of veranda storm lights,
the garden is haunted
by dialling phones and Newton's Cradles,
radios broadcasting static
and the shuffling of worry beads.

The Toy Man

They subvert the shelves
of sales projections and draft brochures
on his sitting room-office wall:
a sniper that clockworks on its belly
through shagpile undergrowth,
a cellophane bird in crisp packet colours
that starts with a twist of its tail.

He settles at the evening table
to a feast of files
and a PC warming up
with the *Mission Impossible* theme:
to hand, a Ribena bulb of wine;
to mouth, a cigarette puffing
like a battery of Airfix artillery.

End and Beginning

When it ended,
we were looking down at the head of the hospital sheet,
where it was still white.

Caroline was kneeling,
turned over by the storm of labour,
her arms an arch to the bedstead.

The midwife placed Eleanor
under us on the bed.
The umbilical twisted from her like a thrown line:

a distance swimmer
greased with vernix
and still panting from her red sea crossing.

Side Order

How many of these side orders of valleys are there,
the lanes only axle-wide necessities
between the business of fields,
the aluminium gates to water meadows
bony as fish spines picked dry?

This meadow has a dead stalk of beech,
snapped off the copse cleanly as celery;
the steep fields are ploughed greedily,
butter-furrowed almost to the hill top;
and the trees fuss, rustling impatiently as waiters.

Kitab suwar al-kawakib
(Book of the Constellations of the Fixed Stars)

The call to prayer dodges street lamps and taxis
to process on our roof, rounding
fat water tanks and cupped satellite dishes,
a/c units shuddering to themselves.

When houses here had to be lifted from the sea
in coral puzzles, they had windtowers that pilfered
breeze from the dhow-braided creek,
smuggled it to majlis and bedrooms.

But when summer's pelt throttled every room,
beds were carried to roofs,
laid beneath *Kitab suwar al-kawakib*'s
spread pages, a mantle light-years deep

seeding through pearls of sweat
dreams of swallowing *The Great Cup*,
dousing under *The Water Carrier*,
plunging from the roof into *The River*.

For Madeleine Mulcahey,
16 July 1998 - 17 December 2000

I have a photograph of my nephew and daughter,
the day after that snow-cushioned funeral:

Richard, in his last slow weeks of fourteen,
is running, left foot on ball-point,
right hand pulling a toboggan's leash;
Alice hunches inside it, exultant in fear.

They are just out of the gate,
Richard in sun,
Alice still clamped in the house's shadow,
ahead, the packed meringue of track.

The image holds them
always at the beginning,
the snow uncut, white coral bushes unshaken,
the brilliance and brittle-bold moment intact.

The Drunk's Stigmata

You spike the slow drinks,
our nights tight as nine pins
on cooling pavements,
air baked to a standstill,
light reluctant to leave
and the confessional quiet
breathing us in one by one,
then out, palms wide as a blessing
and slippery with pints.

You bowl into us slumped,
a man shouldering a beam,
wet thorns in your head
and on your face and knuckles
the drunk's stigmata,
those small scabs you puzzle over
the morning after a lost night.
Swaying, you hold out a palm
and take a collection
for drowning the legion inside you.

Kitchen, 12.07 a.m.

The radio mumbles at the toaster's shoulder.
The striplight hums for the empty house.

I put them to bed, and we – the big-hearted boiler,
my breaths – have the silence to ourselves,

rolling from fields,
night flotsam at the house walls.

The boiler tuts, begins another panting circuit,
lets me off the thought of

something
intruding into the silence

or nothing,
leaving me only to myself.

The boiler, red-eyed, vigilant, takes charge,
hands me up to the bedside radio.

Somewhere There

Where did I lose the blue felt glasses case,
yellow-stitched with my daughter's erratic precision?
It was in my loose pocket

as our party walked Auschwitz,
the mausoleums of hair and shoes, calipers and spectacles,
then the first, workshop, gas chamber.

It was a barb of love
along slide rule tracks
to the chamber-troughs at the birch line.

Even in night returning past The Ramp
where they had separated off the useful,
it was never quite overwhelmed.

Not then, but now I hope, perhaps,
it was not lost on the coach or in my room
or the hotel bar's two-beer sanctuary

but its yellow star-crossings are somewhere
in that choked emptiness, somewhere there
is my daughter's stubborn kindness.

Small Autumn

Our bedroom skylight
looks up at the plane tree lines
of a communal garden.

The leaves stepped down in crowds,
cautious as court shoes,
then long, tip-to-toe strides.

The gardener raked their thin,
open-handed field
into a harvest of pyres.

Tenants walked shoe-box dogs
through gates of the smoke
or watched it break on branches.

Sweet mines of it sank
from glass lips of skylight
onto our hardy, perennial bed.

Smoke Signals

12.11 a.m. and my wife
is reclaiming our bed for sleep.
At 3.30 p.m. we have the clinic:
a curtained wait with just enough
chairs and air for a Consultant
to disburden knowledge, explain
the phone message about my cancer
"progressing a little",
lay out her war on progress.

But now I am hooped between
the kitchen's dozing borders of light.
A glass is unclothing, mouthful
by mouthful of wine, and coaxed
from the chaste tongue of my e-cigarette,
a smoke ring line, skew-whiff hugs,
chasing across the Formica stage.

By the Kitchen Door

For a few seconds two years ago
everything lowered, grew lighter:
standing on warm brick herringbones
between Jamil's forest floor
of vegetables and herbs
and the mango and lemon trees
touching leaves above the washing line,
breeze reaching a mile from the coast
to test the fruit, the afternoon's high Cs
eased to loose pink air.

And sunset's call arriving unexpected
from one minaret, then another, another,
whistles of God swooping like martins
between the shirts' beseeching arms,
bowed over towels
and the socks' applauding line,
a peace unclutchable as a martin
diving to coax shy Jamil's
raygun radishes and sparky rockets from the earth.

Evening Flight, Kingston-London

Sabina Park unfolds in our kitchen strip,
a spinners' wicket twisting through Long Wave static.

Outside, broken snow on dark grass,
like satellite film of Atlantic cloud.

Inside, beamed Jamaican light
eases the timing of ingredients, press of homework.

Tony Cozier describes the Blue Mountains' line
between the worktop and cupboard

turns to six foot seven Sulieman Benn
bowling spin through the doorway

becoming four foot three Benedict
angling in to the biscuit jar

as the ball turns,
pushes on into night.

For Miss Esther Small

The wet Jamaican grass
soaked my canvas shoes
until their cobalt dye
stained me to the ankles.

I stood in the kitchen,
a shoeless white man,
his feet a cold blue
on the warm tiles.

"Now we have to do the rest of you"
Miss Esther said,
black hands poised
across her bleached skirt.

Key to a Map

The stammering footpaths pull your eye
across the dyslexic geometry of fields,
around blue-chip meres and spilling woods.

A séance tap of dead lanes
turning up as potato cobbles under a plough
or leaping the M6 levee between hamlets and barns.

All day the fast lane hums
with ghost herdsmen, labourers, farm hands
vaulting the memory of a stile over cats' eyes.

And all night the same ghosts cross
as suitors, drinkers, poachers
or the booted lay preachers of Northwood Chapel,

returned the cuckoo spit miles from Booth Bank or Lymm,
the Word sown, their hobnails sparking
hard shoulder tongues of fire.

Surprise Incarnation

I ease *100 Baking Recipes from The Co-Op*
from our London dresser like a coin from soil,
its pages sun-crisp
from the '70s Cheshire windowsill.
A cartoon Jon Pertwee (Doctor Who No. 3)
still speech bubbles on the back
about "inner space" and "adventurous meal times".
The cartoon housewife on the cover
still poises a wooden spoon
over her daughter, son and suited husband.
I pick a recipe with my son, harvest ingredients from shelves,
begin, glance at the cover.
That cartoon.

It bundles me into the Tardis,
chucks me back forty years,
I become again
a son in a Cheshire kitchen,
wobbling my pine chair on tiles
as I imagine an adulthood of business-suited glamour –
Old Spice, Rothmans King Size, a Ford Granada.
A pause, enough to remember.
I'm bunged back to London
and showing my son how to pull a wooden spoon
through sandy flapjack weight,
the coming week's business –
school runs, the laundry, adventurous meal times –
whirring in my head.

Two Dreaming Queens

Digging up November soil
I find two sleeping queen bees,
unstained, neat as humbugs,
born at the end of summer
and hibernating until ascension.

I lift them to new soil,
one on a spade, one on a hatchet,

wonder if the two carriages
will insinuate into their dreams,
prepare one for the work
demanded by provision,
the other by succession.

Edward Hopper in Harrogate

The sun is up, a working party
on the abolition of dew,
but Parliament Street is in Boxing Day recess.

Across the way from my window,
and empty as the street,
is a stone Victorian shopfront,
yellow-flushed millstone grit.
Shadows lodge in the bay windows
and mascara the underside of sills.

People passing could see this
as a melancholy Hopper –
a man awake too early,
staring out from his window,
alone with breakfast
and the morning's pallid dish of pills.

They'd pass by, look back down
and never know my delight
at these new blue Christmas pyjamas
at my wife cherishing our duvet
at the shadows' suggestion
of Hopper's *Pennsylvania Coal Town,* 1947,

the man looking up from his rake
at a point beyond his house
in a channel of sun.

High Definition

From his bed our father could hear and see
what we hoped he'd still know as favourite things.
Boogie-woogie and Bach CDs. Test cricket in HD.

The '50s photograph – him a shyly-quiffed RAF Navigator,
the Officers' Mess leather armchairs attained.

The drugs puzzled his descent, comprehension
pain's last theft on the way out. But through the static

clarity, like radio back to base,
bursts, echoing his ascent:

faces shifting as he is passed round aunties in a parlour
paramedics glancing down on the stairs to the flat;

a plum of hand feeling cot blanket fuzz
his praying fingers testing the sheet;

his eyes learning the people who'd become
"Our Dad" and "Mum, love"

his snap of surprise at Siobhan, Claire and me
at the foot of his final bed, then him smiling, saying,
"You three are my children".

Retiring

Somewhere under the lolling grass
of this cart-wide coppice
is Dobb Lane, a Saxon purpose.

But now a harrow
quilts the ground with rust,
a trailer dissolves to crumbs

and as I jog, middle distance oaks
head the rising sun, one to another,
trying to keep it in play.

Tough

That cellar fire
has closed The White Bull until winter,
the pub's glazed look all shuttered up.

HGVs still overnight opposite,
their curtained cribs lay-by mysteries
rocked by the A50's traffic.

And who knows what occurs
behind the boards in that lot by the Bull,
the one where people were growing dope.

Our village does have
oak colonnades on rises, blackberry dips,
cottage bedroom windows open to lane sun.

The pub's sticking front door will reopen,
become again a quickstep across the way
and a moon walk back.

But we'll have to watch the traffic
sliding through, almost seeing
a pub, some houses,

our A road idyll,
patiently siphoning
an almost reluctant love.

Cathedral City

Still shackled to A Levels,
Alice began practising university,
washing knots of clothes,
learning the cost of necessary foods,
unloading on our kitchen top a calculation
of milk, a small loaf, and Cathedral City Cheddar,
knowing she would find its steady block
in her new cathedral city

then head to a checkout queue
that spoke in a different accent,
walk a street just becoming familiar,
resist on unstitching nights the thought
of following the street's Hans Anderson thread
as it spooled from the city
flicked between suburbs, looped cloverleafs,
widened into the M4
blue ribboning back to the kitchen
and its material lines of certainty.

To My Wife, at the Circus

Inside an old chocolate box
in your mother's sideboard,
a Kodak pic 'n' mix:
your sisters as New Romantic scowls,
seaside trips in anoraks,
aunts looking up from laps of cake,
skeleton abbeys,

you,
a teenage precision –
jeans, linen, indifference –
at the age we first met
in that school dance circus of embarrassment.

A corridor from the horror,
your look seemed willing, maybe,
to be half-convinced by me.
And I half saw in you clarity
after the graffiti moods of adolescence

like the detail that brings sense
to a blurry Turner landscape:
the green stroke of a tidal flow,
a red fleck of sun,
white splinters of steel rail
pulling the future close.

The Domesday Book Entry for High Legh Village

It is as simple as notes of sheep wool
across barbed wire staves.
*"Wulfgeat and Dot held it as 2 manors;
they were free men."*
Two manors: even then High Legh carried
the seed of Morse hamlets coded over
a few square arable miles.
*"A priest and a church, with 1 villager
and 2 smallholders."*
You puzzle over a congregation of three
and idle on until ambushed.
*"1 of Gilbert's men has ½ plough
and 3 slaves."*

At seven on Good Friday morning
the A50's air was empty, an almost trucial quiet
over Avenues and Walks in the joggerless estate,
the white Bear's Paw and muckless
converted barns, brown brick cottages
flaunting yellow garden slides,
the bungalows of farmers tired of muck.

A question elbows into the air:
where, in this openness and hedged-about coping,
was the last sentence in the entry?
What would now be choked
by the wood
three miles long, a mile and a half wide,
the trunks pile-driven through kitchens,
branches puncturing poster-covered walls,
thickets upturning Range Rovers,
the canopy's blind migraine?

Keltneyburn Again

For the Mulcaheys

With the sash at half mast
I can hear the River Lyon
over the wet field.

Its slow movement
is unravelling between trees,
a dim magnetic tape

playing rain and the loaded table
past Fortingall, Keltneyburn
and Drummond Hill.

Like every last night here
I memorize the sound
for an aural souvenir,

listening in the trough
of your breaths
to its cold water music

and looking, at your blouse
pole-axed over the iron bedstead
and tights straddling its stile.

Elusive Spin

With raised eyebrows, he says my midlife crisis
has become existential, dodges
a goodnight hug and kiss, grumbles off
past the collage of his growing:
photos of his head sleeping on my shoulder
or him walking, just,
arms reaching.

But before bed, the over
down the long basement corridor,
his bowling arm reaching at me,
the soft indoor ball hugging the mat
for a moment, spinning off,
kissing the bat, stumps,
the bails rising like eyebrows.

Relic

Night presses at the kitchen window,
at the wine glass listening for the table's heart with its
                                        stethoscope,
at the old notebook's spiralled repetition of lists and reminders.

There I find a number in my late father's loose hand,
the lines thin as veins in a petrified leaf.
He'd have written it after the stairs became
a morning and bedtime misadventure
and the leather armchair his all day safe haven.

I still take its memory to bed,
a paper ghost boat carrying me to morning.

From the Tribal Homelands

We scrape off brand labels
in our London sink, white-sticker
maroon-fattened jars –
'Kirkman's Green Damson Jam'.
It's dense as peat, the spoon
spading down, turfing up:

Eleanor reading *Angelina Ballerina*,
legs saluting from the deckchair;
Alice stamping over stocky Cheshire grass
from her cousins' game of rounders;
Benedict prodding bale-thick
hawthorn for a cricket ball.
Around them, fielding memories
of our family plot, the damson trees.

We shake their stumbling rain
from branches into the barrow,
dig out the recipe's hybrid parts,
make identity edible, give it substance
while the children can still taste it:
the chiding-sweet Northern fruit
half soaking our London toast.

Christmas in Isolation

Retoxed,
he swayed by Reception,
an in-out, in-out patient,
his denim stiff as frost,
a blizzard of alcohol,
and flakes of language
a thousand miles from home,
in flight from his mouth.

Out of Touch

Coming back to bed, I close my eyes,
fit my hand between your fingers.
They twitch a puppet show of your dreams,
express things I'll never know.
And good: our children, I,
already crowd your daylight.
It is enough intrusion, enough luck,
that my hand can be a touchpad
for the night language of your fingers,
receive their code, not try to decipher it.

Unfinished Business

The angel on the wall above my desk
was built from driftwood
and her face is blank like a shore stone.
She hangs from a bracket still waiting for a lamp.

The Angel of Incompletion, she bundles under
her unvarnished wing our loose ends –
the unwritten letter that left love messy,
the penalty kick that went wide.

She tuts, regrets,
but won't jump you back
to inspire the neat adieu
or guide the ball to the top corner.

Instead she whispers from her uncut mouth
encouraging doubt:
Did your ex want another letter?
Was it really a foul?

A Taxi Driver Named Ahmed

The dome-minaret, dome-minaret binary code;
neon relish topping burger joints;
the compounds' pale colonies.
And Ahmed's voice.

"I have four sons. I want eight more."
"A cricket team, and a twelfth man?"
"Yes!" A laugh, stumps splayed
around his eyes.

"Where are you from in Pakistan?"
"I come from near the Taliban."
"Is it safe?"
"Yes it is safe."

"The trouble is this much,"
a pinch of lap air between his thumb and forefinger.
"The media make it this much,"
arms spread, the steering wheel riding solo.

The traffic lights' ordered red drops.
*"But we have terrorists –
dirty men, dirty Taliban."*
It detonated from his mouth

and stains the memory of him.
So I back my mind up,
to what Ahmed said
as I leant into the taxi,

"Hello habibi!"
"Hello habibi!"
"Ha! You know what habibi means?"
"Yes, 'Beloved'."

Sanctuary Wood

To reach the wood you pass through
a worn pornography of war:
a room of slick horse tibiae
pulled from the earth, splayed shrapnel,
leather peep-holed cases
to crank through sepia corpses.
The wood's acre,
still scooped from shells,
grassless from tourists' feet
and leaf burst branches,
is a relief, and in wet trenches
fixed in their 11 11 11 weave
you can pity rotting feet
and the necessity of rum.

But for Sanctuary Wood
pornography and pathos alone are too sane.
So next door, 'The Museum',
a tidy 1960s house, gnomes at the porch,
and behind dormer windows in dustless rooms
a masked mannequin child
watches a mannequin Tommy bleed in a bed,
cheery Poilus stab and garrotte Boches
in sunny pastel prints
and the way to the bedrooms is pointed
by serrated bayonets
screwed to floral wallpaper.

Susan on the Wharf

The wharf was on tidal, Hammersmith Thames.
    Susan sold 'confectionery' in Harrods:
It stored cardboard skins creased for boxing,
    brazil nuts in toe-caps of Bourneville;
clean palettes stacked like plates,
    almonds smoking in cocoa;
black machines to heat our night shift.
    a marshmallow crease around her wrist.

We'd smoke behind tarred tanks,
    She'd tip in one extra,
our safety boots on a low wall,
    summersault the plump bag shut,
our eyes on the Harrods Depository,
    and look up, eyes primed with liquorice kohl
its small domes, union flags.
    and mascara crowns of thorn.

Is That the Time Already?

Even after five years,
I can forget the building work:
shuffled rooms surprise me,
the new corridor, flipped staircase.

At the head of the stairs,
four collages I made in spring
of our three children,
glued-down cacophonies,
one hundred and sixty-odd differences.

Each time we made these people,
with no idea of how they'd be,
and we stood drifted together by the hospital liftbank,
our new baby in a car seat,
unreadiness opened
like the greed of air under a rising lift.

I climb the stairs,
hold the still-surprising newel post,
its paint worn through to wood by the children,
their hands on the newel, anchors.

Apart

We tap text, puncture separation
with a line of drill heads: xxxxx

Travelling Companions

A puncture after ten minutes;
time deflating at Kwik Fit.
Then a second pulling away,
the retread of emotion through home streets,
dark moving into second gear,
the cord from family stretched
at every green light.

Loading the car, I'd bounced
my son's two taut footballs
from the boot onto the back shelf.
All through the motorway night
they tapped together-apart
in the rear-view mirror:
a cartoon of bickering children,
a rolling, surreal comfort.

Why do I need the comfort?
My wife, our children,
annexed my soul last century.
But our flat's high cupboards
are blocked with old baby clothes;
my daughter's friendship bracelet
loops coins in the desk drawer.

Threading from Warwick Services,
half way apart,
the footballs jostle again,
continue to the empty house where I grew up.
Lights are on. Why?
Last week, thieves were here,
taking flagstones my father laid
with cement-cratered fingers
on '70s slab weekends,

peeling an imagined safe skin
from the house.
I replace it in my mind
with the footballs' soft armour plate
as they settle on the shelf
against the black garden,
substitutes coming late in the game,
spare, defensive comfort.

Restoring Balance

That month was swaddled in frost.
The builders paused at the bonfire's whitened timbers
and their boots minted the grass
on the way back to the old pig sty and privy.
The new feather slates and denture bricks
fixed in the memory of our house as a smallholding,
of work ploughing boundaries around Victorian weeks,
the close fields mapped onto palms.

And in the bonfire's ash plate,
bottle chunks, the crusted privy latch, meaty lips of bowl,
a debris of cramped lives.
But, in spring, an uncertain expanse,
crockery peering up from soil at the sty's mouth.
Vines and cobalt on farthing-width china.
A scimitar of port wine glass clear as dimpled air.

I brushed the soil off, as they did:
best china and port wine at Christenings
to cleanse the siege of fields and earth;
cobalt side plates for a friend flickering
past windows to the back door bearing cake;
a wedge Sunday ox tongue sticking out
from a vine-patterned dish at the gathering week.

San Trovarso, Venice, in the District of Dorsoduro

The concierge in San Marco
was a pursed severity, too busy
for honeymooners' suitcases.
We lurched up sharp flights
to a roofscape bullied by bells.
Our children climb with us now,
three stories in Dorsoduro,
a stumbling of headphones, keys, wheelies,
twenty-five years of marriage, crisps.

Stretching the last glass I watch
boats mutter home. Students glide
the moulting piazza.
Across locked hulls is San Trovarso,
heavy-shouldered, braced
with candles and kneelers
for whatever cargo of souls washes up.

The church was a box of agreed peace
between the working clans of Venice.
The Nicolotti used the west door,
the Castellani the south.
Faces recognised across an aisle
from the autumn battles on bridges in truce
until the priest's final warning to "Ite in pace".

They genuflected on the squat-cross floor.
Dipped their splinters in the granite stoup.
Looked around the warehouse-high walls
and perhaps saw themselves
in the Tintoretto Last Supper:
the disciples' weary clothes, generations
labouring around a cramped table.